TODAY'S GREAT QUARTERBACKS

ROBERT GRIFFIN III

By Ryan Nagelhout

Gareth Stevens
Publishing

Right On!

Please visit our website www.garethstevens.com. For a free color catalog of all our high-quality books, call toll free 1-800-542-2595 or fax 1-877-542-2596.

Library of Congress Cataloging-in-Publication Data

Nagelhout, Ryan.
Robert Griffin III / by Ryan Nagelhout.
  p. cm. — (Today's great quarterbacks)
Includes index.
ISBN 978-1-4824-0484-5 (pbk.)
ISBN 978-1-4824-0485-2 (6-pack)
ISBN 978-1-4824-0482-1 (library binding)
1. Griffin, Robert, — III, — 1990- — Juvenile literature. 2. Football players — United States — Biography — Juvenile literature. 3. Quarterbacks (Football) — United States — Biography — Juvenile literature. I. Nagelhout, Ryan. II. Title.
GV939.G775 N34 2014
796.332092—dc23

First Edition

Published in 2014 by
Gareth Stevens Publishing
111 East 14th Street, Suite 349
New York, NY 10003

Designer: Nicholas Domiano
Editor: Ryan Nagelhout

Photo credits: Cover, p. 1 Win McNamee/Getty Images Sport/Getty Images; p. 5 Kevin Mazur/WireImage/Getty Images; p. 7 Jamie Squire/Getty Image Sport/Getty Images; pp. 9, 23 Patrick McDermott/Getty Image Sport/Getty Images; p. 11 John McDonnell/The Washington Post/Getty Images; p. 13 Sarah Glenn/Getty Images Sport/Getty Images; p. 15 Brian Bahr/Getty Images Sport/Getty Images; pp. 17, 25 Ronald Martinez/Getty Images Sport/Getty Images; p. 19 Jeff Zelevansky/Getty Images Sport/Getty Images; p. 21 Al Bello/Getty Images Sport/Getty Images; p. 27 Jeffrey Ufberg/WireImage/Getty Images; p. 29 Kevin C. Cox/Getty Images Sport/Getty Images.

CPSIA compliance information: Batch #CW14GS: For further information contact Gareth Stevens, New York, New York at 1-800-542-2595.

CONTENTS

Meet Robert

Robert Griffin III is a great quarterback. He's a star in the **National Football League** (NFL).

Robert Lee Griffin III was born February 12, 1990, in Okinawa, Japan. His parents, Jacqueline and Robert Jr., were both in the US Army.

Traveling Griffins

Robert's family moved a lot. He grew up in Tacoma, Washington, and New Orleans, Louisiana. He went to high school in Copperas Cove, Texas.

Robert loved to run! He ran track
and played basketball and football.
People said he was the fastest kid
at his high school!

College Quarterback

Many **colleges** wanted Robert to play football for them. Most wanted him to play wide receiver or defensive back. He decided to go to Baylor University and play quarterback instead.

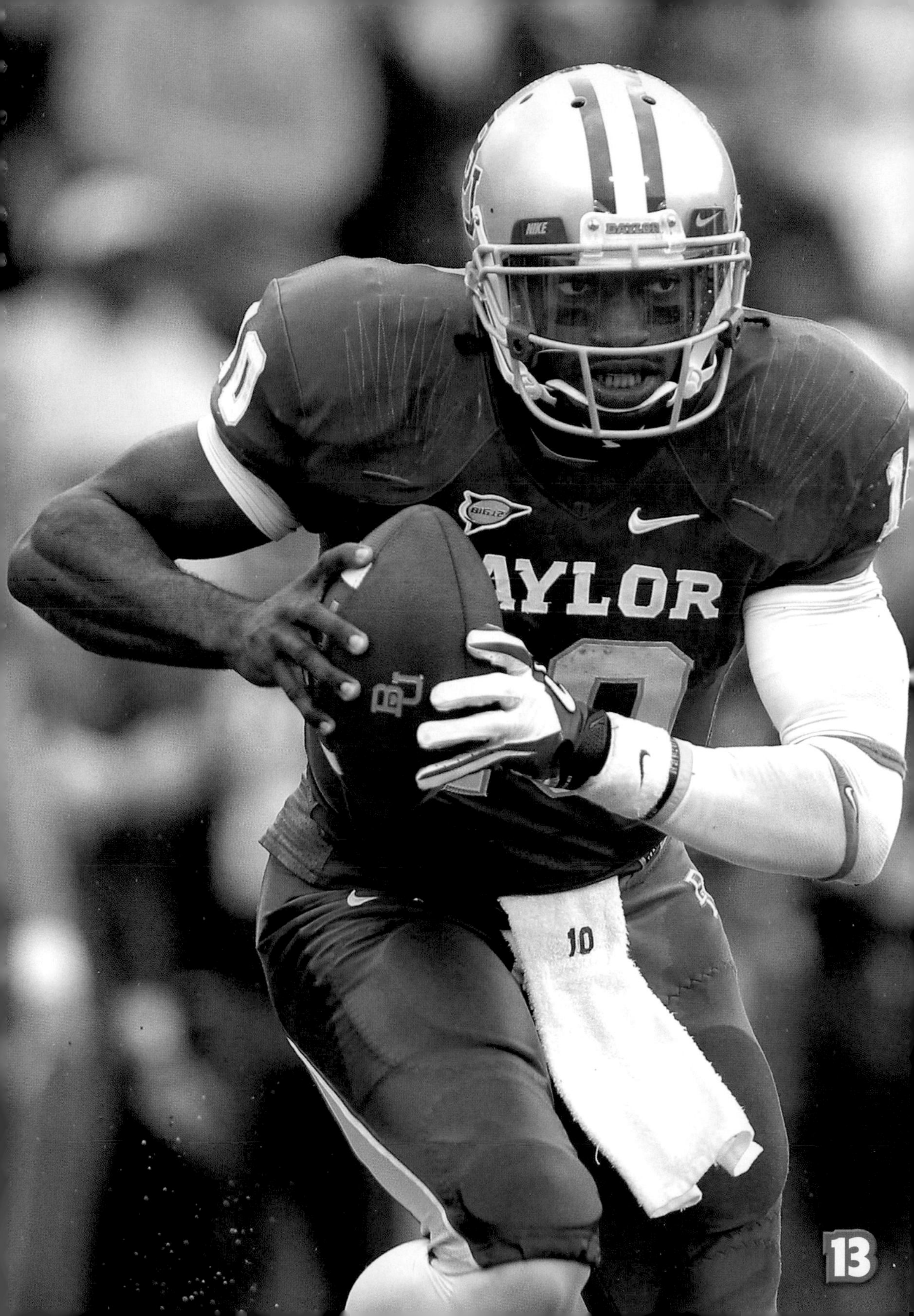
BAYLOR
NIKE
AYLOR
10

The Nickname

Robert wore "Griffin III" on his jersey in college. That's where his nickname "RG3" came from. Some people call his dad "RG2"!

RG3 played very well for the Baylor Bears. He set or tied 54 school records in 41 games. He helped Baylor win its first bowl game in more than 20 years!

Heisman Honors

In 2012, Robert won the Heisman **Trophy**. It's given to the best player in college football. RG3 decided he was going pro.

Robert was picked by Washington second overall in the 2012 NFL **Draft**. Washington traded the St. Louis Rams for the pick. They really liked Robert!

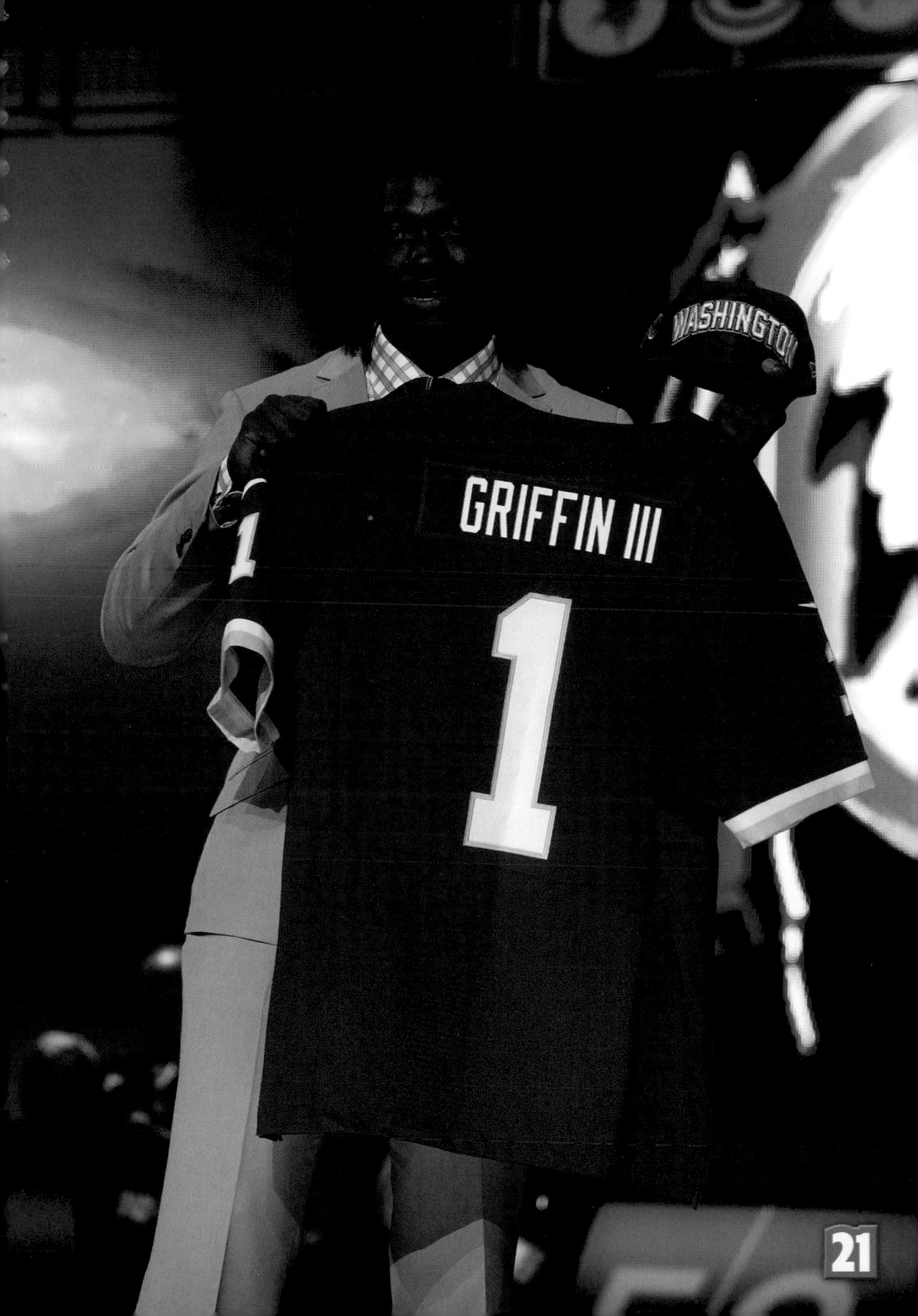
WASHINGTON
GRIFFIN III
1

The Rookie

Robert had an amazing **rookie** season with Washington. He led his team to a division title. They also made the playoffs.

Robert won the Offensive Rookie of the Year award. He beat out rookie quarterbacks like Indianapolis's Andrew Luck and Seattle's Russell Wilson for the honor. He also made the Pro Bowl!

Star Socks

One day in high school, Robert wore a red sock with a blue sock. He became known for his colorful socks. Today, he sells his own line of socks!

What's Next?

RG3's career is just getting started.

What will he do next?

Timeline

1990   Robert Griffin III is born February 12.

2006   Robert starts at quarterback for Copperas Cove High School.

2008   Robert goes to Baylor University to play football and run track.

2012   Robert wins Heisman Trophy.

   RG3 drafted by Washington.

2013   Robert leads Washington to the playoffs.

   RG3 wins NFL Offensive Rookie of the Year award.

For More Information

Books

Bodden, Valerie. *Robert Griffin III*. Mankato, MN: Creative Education, 2013.

Graves, Will. *RGIII–NFL Sensation*. Minneapolis, MN: ABDO Publishing, 2014.

Websites

RGIII's Heisman Trophy Website

bu-rg3.com

Find out more about Griffin's college career on this site.

Robert Griffin's NFL Player Profile

nfl.com/player/robertgriffiniii/2533033/profile

See Robert's stats, highlights, and more on his official player page.

Publisher's note to educators and parents: Our editors have carefully reviewed these websites to ensure that they are suitable for students. Many websites change frequently, however, and we cannot guarantee that a site's future contents will continue to meet our high standards of quality and educational value. Be advised that students should be closely supervised whenever they access the Internet.

Glossary

college: a school after high school

draft: a way to pick new football players for NFL teams

National Football League: the top football league in the United States

rookie: a first-year player in professional sports

trophy: a prize given for winning something

Index